PUBLIC RECORD OFFICE

IMAGES OF WAR
BRITISH POSTERS 1939-45

John D Cantwell

London Her Majesty's Stationery Office

ISBN 0 11 440221 3

British Library Cataloguing in
Publication Data
A CIP catalogue record for this book is
available from the British Library

HMSO
BOOKS

HMSO publications are available from:

HMSO Publications Centre
  (Mail and telephone orders only)
PO Box 276, London, SW8 5DT
Telephone orders 01-873 9090
General enquiries: 01-873 0011
(queuing system in operation for
both numbers)

HMSO Bookshops
49 High Holborn, London, WC1V 6HB   01-873 0011
(Counter service only)
258 Broad Street, Birmingham, B1 2HE   021-643 3740
Southey House, 33 Wine Street, Bristol, BS1 2BQ   (0272) 264306
9-21 Princess Street, Manchester, M60 8AS   061-834 7201
80 Chichester Street, Belfast, BT1 4JY   (0232) 238451
71 Lothian Road, Edinburgh, EH3 9AZ   031-228 4181

HMSO's Accredited Agents
(see Yellow Pages)

And through good booksellers

Printed in the United Kingdom for
Her Majesty's Stationery Office
Dd 240449   C90   9/89   12521

Contents

No British poster of the Second World War had the dramatic impact or the enduring quality of Kitchener's 'Your Country Needs YOU' in the First. Yet for millions of Britons who lived through the war years from 1939 to 1945, such poster themes as 'Dig for Victory', 'Careless talk costs lives' and 'Is your journey really necessary?' were never to be forgotten. Hitler's infamies had united the people so the nation was ready to respond to the call to arms. Women willingly served as actively as men, not only by joining the auxiliary forces, but also by taking up work on the land, in civil defence, the fire brigade or as members of the Women's Voluntary Service. But until Churchill became prime minister and formed a coalition government in May 1940, the country lacked resolute leadership. Early publicity on the Home Front reflected that uncertainty, and the first tentative efforts of the Ministry of Information, which was responsible for propaganda, have already been critically documented in a previous Public Record Office book *This is your war* (HMSO, 1983).

The wartime posters reproduced in this publication are but a small selection from the many hundreds prepared. Visually, they cannot be regarded as great works of art; neither were they intended as such by the artists concerned, many of them already distinguished within their own profession. But besides their message they tell us something of the prevailing manners and customs. They also mirror the changing fortunes of the war, as may be seen from the short account which follows of the events leading up to its outbreak in 1939 and its course thereafter.

At daybreak on 1 September 1939 the German army entered Poland on Adolf Hitler's orders. Germany had been harshly treated after losing the First World War. The peace treaty she had been made to sign at Versailles in 1919 was meant, in the words of the popular slogan, to squeeze her until the pips squeaked. Protests of economists, such as Keynes, were brushed aside. Predictably, it caused grave economic difficulties for the Germans, which were made worse when a world slump occurred in 1929 in the wake of the Wall Street crash. The resulting leap in unemployment was an important factor in helping Hitler's National Socialist (Nazi) party to gain power in 1933.

Hitler traded also on German resentment about the lands it had been made to surrender after the 1914-18 war, and the existence of German minorities in the newly independent states of Czechoslovakia and Poland. In 1936 Hitler reoccupied the demilitarised Rhineland, and in March 1938 he annexed Austria, the Germanic nerve centre of the former Austro-Hungarian empire. Later that year the Czechs lost the Sudetenland after Neville Chamberlain, the British prime minister, backed by France, had flown to Munich to avert war by settling the crisis on Hitler's terms, believing it the last of his territorial demands. Momentarily, it seemed that Chamberlain's appeasement policy (or buying time, as some have later argued) had been vindicated, but Hitler had no intention of keeping his word. By March 1939 Czechoslovakia had been dismembered, German troops had occupied Prague, and the huge Skoda arms factory was in their hands.

In Germany Hitler's persecution of the Jews, which was to end in the horror of the Holocaust, was being intensified, and he was already making threatening noises about the Poles. The Versailles treaty gave them access to the Baltic Sea by the grant of a corridor through East Prussia. To reclaim that strip and to annex the 'free city' of Danzig (now Gdansk), Hitler launched his forces in a *blitzkrieg* ('lightning war') against Poland, having first cleared the way by signing a non-aggression pact with Russia in August 1939. Five months earlier a by then disillusioned Chamberlain had given Poland a guarantee of support if her independence was threatened and she felt obliged to resist. Right up to the last moment Chamberlain hoped that the Poles might negotiate, but on 3 September, two days after Hitler had struck, he told the nation in a radio broadcast that, all attempts at settlement having failed, Britain was at war with Germany. That same afternoon the French, even more hesitantly, declared likewise.

But Britain and France were in no position to give swift military help to the Poles, whose plight was made worse when the Russians, taking advantage of the situation, moved in from the east on 17 September. By the end of the month Poland had ceased to exist, being partitioned by agreement between Germany and Russia. In fact, the Polish offensive was only part of Hitler's longer-term aim for more living space ('lebensraum') for the German people by a drive to the east. Fearful for its borders Russia had no compunction about compelling its pre-1914 to 1918 Baltic provinces to allow military bases in their territories. Estonia, Latvia and Lithuania submitted, and were later to be incorporated in the Soviet Union. However, Finland refused to acquiesce and gave way in March 1940 only after it had fought a valiant military campaign. Its stand was greatly admired by Britain and France, who might well have become fatally embroiled had the Finns not sought terms.

In Britain the outbreak of war with Germany, unlike in 1914, had not been accompanied by a wild display of public enthusiasm. The onslaught anticipated from the air was too greatly dreaded for that, and the mood of the people was sombre and determined. In expectation of the havoc to come, the government had laid plans for children to be evacuated from the major cities, and they were now sent to areas thought safe from bombing. When, at first, air raids failed to materialise, parents who were tempted to bring their

National Service Acts

IMPORTANT NOTICE TO APPRENTICES AND LEARNERS

If you wish to complete your apprentice-ship or similar training before you are called-up, you should apply immediately for deferment of call-up.

A form of application (N.S. 294) can be obtained at this office.

N.S. 7

Wt. T16560/1575 350 4/40 CN&CoLtd 740 (5577)

Young men learning a trade were among the few categories who could have their call-up to the Forces deferred.
LAB 45/81

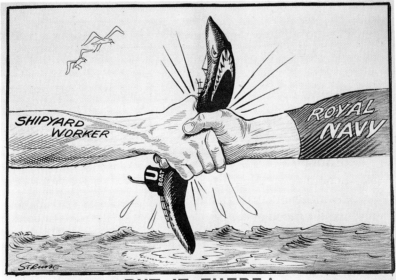

SHIPYARD WORKER

ROYAL NAVY

U BOAT

Strube

PUT IT THERE!

Put It There
Artist: Strube
Printer: H Manly & Son
Ltd, London
$26\frac{1}{4}$" x $19\frac{3}{4}$"
INF 13/122/19

When gardening is done	No.	%
Mornings	81	2.9
Afternoons	75	2.7
Evenings	1027	36.7
Week-ends	511	18.2
Sundays	238	8.5
Spare Time	1114	39.8
Plenty of Time	320	11.4
$\frac{1}{2}$ days, holidays	76	2.7
Full time Gardener	24	.8
Saturday	110	3.9
TOTAL	2801	127.6

In 1942 the Wartime Social Survey carried out an inquiry for the Ministry of Agriculture into the effects of the 'Dig for Victory' campaign. This table shows that most of those questioned did their gardening in their spare time — which they did not specify — or in the evenings. Television was not a distraction in those days.
RG 23/26, p35

children back had to be cautioned against doing so by the Ministry of Health, which as the successor of the old Local Government Board was responsible for local authority welfare services. Besides the exodus of schoolchildren and mothers with young families, many government offices left London, involving the Office of Works in the wholesale requisitioning of properties to house the staff concerned — much to the dismay of the hoteliers and others affected, although they received compensation, with provision for the settlement of disputes through a General Claims Tribunal. The most prized contents of vulnerable museums and art galleries were also removed, and similar action was taken to transport the more important classes of public records to country repositories.

Men aged between 18 and 41 could be conscripted into the forces, and compulsion was complemented by voluntary recruitment campaigns. Apart from those in reserved occupations, medically unfit or with a conscientious objection to the bearing of arms, it was possible to be excused military service by opting to work in the mines. Few did so, with the result that in 1943 a system of balloting took place whereby ten per cent of conscripts were sent to the pits — 'Bevin boys' as they were known. Efforts were also made to recruit women into the services. In the country at large everyone was registered and given an identity card soon after war began, as a prelude to food rationing. The urgent need for such a scheme, which was introduced early in 1940, could not be doubted because from the very outset of war British merchant ships, bringing in food and essential supplies, came under fierce attack, mainly from U-boats. On the first day of the war the liner *Athenia* was torpedoed with the loss of 112 lives, and by the end of 1939 the Germans had sunk over 100 ships. The convoy system, which had saved Britain in the First World War, was hampered by a shortage of escort vessels, and had yet to be fully developed. It was hardly surprising that the early posters

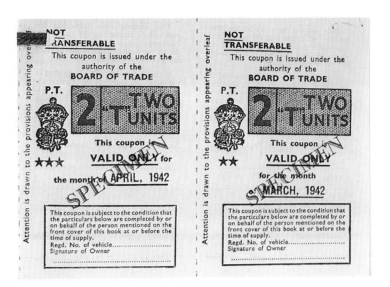

Specimen petrol coupon supplied to provincial taxi drivers.
POWE 33/1441

placed so much emphasis upon food production and getting in the harvest. Throughout the war much attention was given to the economical use of food.

At first all was quiet on the Western Front, the French and British forces being content to remain in what was thought to be the safety of the Maginot Line. Opposite them stood the enemy's Siegfried Line, while at home the audiences in the variety halls sang:

We're gonna hang out the washing on the Siegfried Line,
Have you any dirty washing, Mother dear?
We're gonna hang out the washing on the Siegfried Line,
'Cos the washing day is here.

By contrast the war at sea, like the brutal conquest of Poland, was real enough, but the absence of any large-scale fighting on land between the Great Powers led to the period being dubbed the 'Phoney War' or, in Germany, *Sitzkrieg* (the 'Sitting Down War'). Yet in the towns the balloon barrage, sandbagged buildings, camouflaged factories and the carrying of gas masks were a constant reminder of the perils expected from the sky. The night-time blackout was at that time a bigger threat to personal safety, particularly on the roads, than Hitler's bombers, lessened only slightly when the number of vehicles in use was reduced by the introduction of petrol rationing a few weeks after war started. The *Luftwaffe* was too busily engaged in Poland to respond immediately to a somewhat ineffectual daylight raid by the RAF on 4 September on enemy warships at Wilhelmshaven. In October, however, the daring sinking by a U-boat of the battleship *Royal Oak* at Scapa Flow was followed by an attack by a small force of bombers upon naval ships in the Firth of Forth. Fortunately, no great harm was done, but the Germans secured a strategic victory because the Admiralty felt obliged to move the bulk of the home fleet to the less convenient west coast of Scotland until the eastern defences could be strengthened. British pride was partially

'BACK ROOM BOYS'

'THEY ALSO SERVE'

Issued in 1942. Although women were prominent in industry this poster does not suggest that the underlying attitude towards them had changed.
AN 2/788

restored in December when the German surface raider, the pocket battleship *Admiral Graf Spee,* was scuttled in the River Plate, having been forced into Montevideo after a fight with British cruisers. The Royal Navy had further success when the German supply ship *Altmark* was boarded in a Norwegian fjord in February 1940, and nearly 300 British prisoners, who had been taken from sunken merchant ships, were released from captivity.

That episode highlighted for Hitler the threat to his Swedish supplies of iron ore, essential for armaments manufacture, which during the winter months went by rail to the Norwegian port of Narvik and were shipped to Germany from there. Primarily to safeguard that traffic he invaded Norway in April, 1940, taking over Denmark in the process. Britain and France were already planning extensive minelaying operations in Norwegian waters and immediately sent in troops, but failed to make headway. Chamberlain paid the price, losing the confidence of a large number of his fellow Conservatives, and was succeeded by Churchill. Further heavy blows were to follow. That May the Germans invaded the Low Countries, outflanking the Maginot Line. No sooner had Belgium and Holland been overrun than Mussolini's Italy entered the war on Hitler's side. Still worse, France collapsed in June. Mercifully, most of the British Expeditionary Force managed to escape — notably from Dunkirk, thanks to the help of an armada of little ships and boats. It was joined in Britain by thousands of Belgians, Czechs, Danes, Dutchmen, Norwegians and Poles, who were determined to fight on under the banners of their governments-in-exile. A strong Free French contingent under General De Gaulle was also making its presence felt, having nothing but contempt for the aged Petain's Vichy goverment which had capitulated to Hitler.

Ministry of Information booklet, issued in 1943.
INF 2/3, p.112

THE
HOME GUARD
OF BRITAIN

At this dark hour the Home Guard, later to be satirised as 'Dad's Army', was formed. Invasion was feared at any moment, and there was a drive against aliens and those suspected of Fascist leanings or being spies — the Fifth Column. Some were wrongly imprisoned and even the courts were hard pushed to protect them under the draconian powers vested in the home secretary under Defence Regulation 18B. One case of doubtful legality, *Liversidge v. Anderson,* which went in favour of the Crown after being taken to the House of Lords, was subsequently to be known as their lordships' contribution to the war effort. But apprehension about the enemy within was widespread, and posters emphasising the need to guard against careless talk began to appear, as did the slogan 'Be like Dad, keep Mum'. Its display aroused no great resentment, yet today it seems as fatuous as another, which might have come from Berlin itself, illustrating German uniforms so that the public might 'spot them at sight'. But some minds were already working on the assumption that attack was the best form of defence. Among them was Admiral of the Fleet Sir Roger Keyes, of First World War Zeebrugge fame, who was appointed Director of Combined Operations by Churchill to launch commando raids against German-occupied territory. Keyes did not stay long, but the formation of the new force was an important factor in raising morale and an aid to the campaign to hit back by more production in which the role of women was increasingly stressed. Even so, a set of London Transport posters featuring women workers still appeared under the heading 'Backroom Boys'.

The German plan to invade had broken down after the *Luftwaffe's* failure to win air supremacy in the Battle of Britain, which was fought with the Hurricanes and Spitfires of the RAF between August and September 1940. Tactically, the battle was lost when the Germans, having stretched the defenders almost to their limit, made the mistake of switching their attack from the airfields to London. The British radar chain, even more than its Observer Corps, was a key factor in the successful defence. Additionally, the possession, unknown to the Germans, of a decoding machine ('Ultra') which enabled their wireless communications to be read, was of great assistance. But these technical aids in no way detracted from the great bravery of the RAF fighter pilots, including a strong Polish element, immortalised in Churchill's famous words 'Never in the field of human conflict was so much owed by so many to so few.'

Throughout the winter of 1940-41 German bombers pounded British cities in night-time raids against which there was no adequate defence at that time. London bore the brunt of it, but Birmingham, Bristol, Coventry, Glasgow, Liverpool and Plymouth were among those which also suffered severely. Most people stayed in their own homes, moving to their 'Anderson' air-raid shelter in their garden or 'Morrison' shelter under the table when danger seemed imminent. Others took refuge in the underground railway stations. The biggest menace came from incendiary bombs and every neighbourhood had its air-raid wardens and firewatch patrols. Despite the appalling plight of those who lost their homes morale stood up remarkably well, perhaps because even worse had been feared. Many of the older men had served in the trenches during the First World War, and their calmness under bombardment was a factor of key importance. Government publicity concentrated upon how to combat the attacks through firefighting, and made much of the way the RAF was hitting back. Local authorities made arrangements to find accommodation for the homeless, and a scheme of compensation in respect of land and buildings was operated by a War Damage Commission. Compensation for personal belongings, however, rested with the Board of Trade. To avoid the stigma of bankruptcy those whose businesses or private affairs ran into financial difficulties as a result of the war were enabled to make arrangements with their creditors through officers attached to the county courts under the Liabilities (War-Time Adjustment) Acts 1941 and 1944. The enormous cost of financing the war meant that great emphasis was placed upon the importance of national savings. 'Lend to

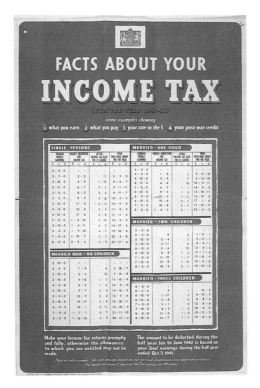

Left   **Facts About Your Income Tax**
Printer: Brent Press Ltd, London
29¾″ x 19¾″
IR 78/7

Bottom left   As hospital work was vital, the Ministry of Labour and National Service emphasised to health service workers the importance of staying in post.
MH 101/9

Below   Fruit juices, cod liver oil and vitamin tablets were made available at local Food Offices and Welfare Centres.
MAF 102/81

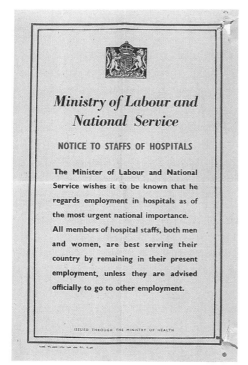

Boys and girls aged 16 to 18 had to fill in this card under the youth registration scheme. If not already undertaking training or service they were interviewed so that they might be helped to do their 'duty as a citizen' and 'assist the present national effort'.
ED 124/46

REGISTRATION OF BOYS AND GIRLS ORDER, 1941

1. Full Name (Surname in block letters)	7. If attending evening classes, state name of school or evening institute
Surname	
Other	
Names	
2. National Registration Identity Card No.	8. If in employment state : (a) Present occupation
	(b) Name and address of present employer : Name
3. Address (in full)	Address
	(c) Business of employer
4. Delete Male or Female	5. Date of Birth	*9. If a member of any Youth Organisation (including Civil Defence Organisations) and/or of a Pre-Service Training Organisation (Home Guard, Sea Cadets, Army Cadets or A.T.C.) state :— (a) Name of Organisation : (b) Address of Unit :
6. If attending full-time educational course, state name of school or other educational establishment.	(a) Name of Organisation : (b) Address of Unit :
	*NOTE :—Where a boy or girl is a member of more than one Organisation particulars should be entered of each Organisation (whether Youth Organisation or Pre-Service Organisation).

E.D. 431   M17243 500M 8-42 CN&Co. 749

Defend the Right to be Free'. Inevitably, taxation ran at a high level. Purchase tax, the forerunner of VAT, was in force from 1940 and a PAYE scheme for the collection of income tax was announced in that same year, but did not become fully operational until 1944. The need to tighten up was signalled also by clothes rationing, introduced in 1941, and an intensification of the various salvage and fuel-saving campaigns. The general austerity was reflected in the production of furniture to utility standards, and 'British Restaurants', run by local authorities in church halls and the like, appeared in the cities. The surroundings were spartan but the food, while plain, was welcome to those unable to get home for a midday meal or without a canteen. An Emergency Hospital Scheme and a Blood Transfusion Service were in operation and much attention was given to health propaganda, 'coughs and sneezes spread diseases' being perhaps the best-known advice. Likewise, extra food and vitamins were provided for expectant mothers and small children. Some increase in venereal diseases also led to the display of cautionary posters about a previously taboo subject. In an effort to direct young people into useful activity, registration was undertaken of those between the ages of 16 to 18, and those unattached to any youth or pre-service organisation were interviewed and encouraged to join a suitable club, association or unit.

Britain's determination to fight on was undoubted, surrender being unthinkable. In an extremity Churchill and his Cabinet would have fought on from Canada or elsewhere. But until the middle of 1941 the country stood alone, apart from the loyal support of the Dominions and Free European forces. It was not surprising that Hitler, having by then extended his conquests by subjugating Yugoslavia and Greece and taking Crete (after a brave fight by British, Australian and New Zealand troops) was in confident mood. At any rate, in June 1941 he felt sufficiently secure in the west to launch the invasion of Russia he had long been

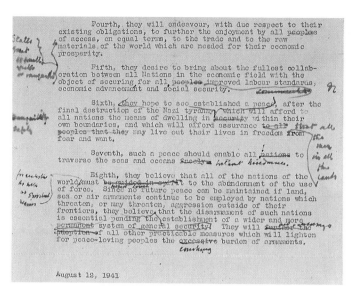

Fourth, they will endeavour, with due respect to their
existing obligations, to further the enjoyment by all peoples
of access, on equal terms, to the trade and to the raw
materials of the world which are needed for their economic
prosperity.

Fifth, they desire to bring about the fullest collab-
oration between all Nations in the economic field with the
object of securing for all peoples improved labour standards,
economic advancement and social security.

Sixth, they hope to see established a peace, after the
final destruction of the Nazi tyranny which will afford to
all nations the means of dwelling in security within their
own boundaries, and which will afford assurance to all
peoples that they may live out their lives in freedom from
fear and want.

Seventh, such a peace should enable all nations to
traverse the seas and oceans freely without hindrance.

Eighth, they believe that all of the nations of the
world must be guided in spirit to the abandonment of the use
of force. Since no future peace can be maintained if land,
sea or air armaments continue to be employed by nations which
threaten, or may threaten, aggression outside of their
frontiers, they believe that the disarmament of such nations
is essential pending the establishment of a wider and more
permanent system of general security. They will further the
adoption of all other practicable measures which will lighten
for peace-loving peoples the excessive burden of armaments.

August 12, 1941

Section of 'Atlantic Charter', 12 August 1941. The amendments are Churchill's.
FO 371/28903, f1936

planning. Some weeks before, his deputy, Rudolph Hess, made a sensational flight from Germany and landed in Scotland, not far from the home of the Duke of Hamilton, carrying proposals for a peace settlement. The full story of that bizarre episode has yet to be told, but it seems that Hess (if it was Hess as some have questioned) was acting independently. If he was hoping for Britain to join in a crusade against Russia he was soon disappointed because Churchill, despite his robust anti-Communism, was clear that Russia had to be sustained, and many British lives and ships were lost in carrying supplies to its Arctic ports. Stalin, the Russian leader, urged the creation of a second front but that was not immediately practicable — a large-scale raid against Dieppe in 1942, in which the Canadians suffered appalling losses, had made it evident that more time and preparation were needed.

Meanwhile, across the Atlantic, President Roosevelt had been responsible for lend-leasing ships and munitions to Britain, but he had to move cautiously because isolationism was still a powerful force in America. In August 1941 he met Churchill on a ship near Newfoundland and they jointly agreed upon an 'Atlantic Charter', foreshadowing the principles upon which the United Nations Organisation was to be founded in 1945. The president's dilemma was solved when Japan, which had previously pledged itself to support its Axis partners, Germany and Italy, if the USA took up arms against them, decided to get the first blow in by a surprise attack upon Pearl Harbor from the air in December 1941, in which they inflicted terrible damage upon the American fleet. In the months that followed, British and Australian forces in Malaya and Singapore were overwhelmed by the Japanese, and Hong Kong and the Dutch East Indies also fell. Before long the Japanese were pushing through Burma to the Indian border, and the north Australian port of Darwin was being bombed from New Guinea. It was a bad time for Britain which also suffered reverses in

Africa, where German and Italian forces under Rommel had taken the key stronghold of Tobruk. At home Churchill survived a vote of confidence, and in October 1942 the tide began to turn when Montgomery's Eighth Army decisively defeated Rommel at the battle of El Alamein.

Of equal importance the ceaseless war against the U-boats in the Atlantic was beginning to move in favour of the allies, and the development of a new radar detection device prevented Doenitz's submarines from operating as an effective force from the middle of 1943. Germany was now on the defensive, its army having suffered a crushing defeat at the hands of the Russians at Stalingrad. In the Mediterranean, Sicily and southern Italy had been occupied by Anglo/American forces. Mussolini had been overthrown but remained defiant, having been rescued from captivity by German paratroopers. However, the new Italian government surrendered and was soon to change sides. A bomber offensive against Germany was now taking a terrible toll of its cities, although the allied air forces were suffering increasingly heavy losses as the Germans improved their defences. Germany was too preoccupied in the east to carry out other than spasmodic air attacks against Britain. In 1942, however, there had been a series of what were called 'Baedeker' raids against British towns of historical importance architecturally, such as Bath, Canterbury, Exeter, Norwich and York.

In German-occupied territories the European resistance movement was gaining strength with backing from Britain's Special Operations Executive (SOE) and the dropping of airborne supplies. Yugoslav partisans, under Tito, were especially active. In Britain itself all-out preparations were being made for the invasion of the continent, giving point to the renewed campaign to discourage public travel and the declaration of areas to which entry was restricted. On D-Day, 6 June 1944, the allied armies made a successful landing in Normandy, under the supreme command of

General Eisenhower. The expedition, 'Operation Overlord', was the greatest seaborne operation in history and brilliantly succeeded in establishing a bridgehead for the liberating armies, partly because the Germans had been led by British intelligence to expect a landing in the area of Calais. Shortly afterwards a new hazard arose for the British people when Hitler unleashed unmanned flying bombs (V1s), better known as doodlebugs, and rockets (V2s) against London and the home counties. Much damage and many casualties were caused by these terrifying weapons before their launching pads were overrun by the invading allied armies.

In the cities, a start was being made to rehouse the homeless, and prefabricated dwellings ('prefabs') began to fill the sites cleared by bombing. Although they were ugly to look at they were to prove popular with their tenants. In Germany a group of German officers and patriots made an unsuccessful attempt to assassinate Hitler in July 1944, and fearful reprisals were to follow against them. One of those on the periphery of the conspiracy was none other than Rommel, who opted to take poison rather than stand trial. In Holland a British airborne assault at Arnheim in September 1944 met with disaster, but the end of the tyrant's reign could not long be delayed. On the eastern front the German army was in full retreat and Hitler, caught between the pursuing Russians and the allied powers from the west, and with his empire crumpling around him, died by his own hand on 30 April 1945 in his Berlin bunker, along with his companion Eva Braun. Two days earlier, Mussolini had been seized with his mistress at Como by Italian partisans and both were brutally executed. Only the account with the Japanese remained to be settled, and the British felt sufficiently relaxed to revert to peacetime habits by holding the general election delayed by the war. The country was in a mood for change, and in July Churchill was replaced by a Labour government, headed by Attlee, who had loyally and ably served as his deputy since 1940. Shortly afterwards Japan surrendered, after atomic bombs were dropped by the Americans on Hiroshima and Nagasaki. These dreadful weapons of mass destruction had been developed in America in great secrecy by the allies, British and European nuclear scientists prominent among them.

In Britain the end of fighting was greeted as much with relief as with jubilation. Ever since America entered the war Churchill had been confident of ultimate victory. Much planning had been undertaken for the work of reconstruction in the postwar world, although it was not directly reflected in government publicity because it was thought to contain the seeds of party political conflict. Nevertheless, even before the coalition government broke up, a new Education Act was passed in 1944, and a revolutionary measure providing for the payment of family allowances was placed on the statute book in 1945. Town and country planning was in the hands of a new ministry and schemes had been drawn up to designate national parks and areas of natural beauty. Above all, the Beveridge Report of 1942, with its attack upon the five giant evils of Want, Disease, Ignorance, Squalor and Idleness, was seen as the blueprint for the brave new world it was hoped to build. More prosaically, the social revolution could be seen as the flowering of a process of state involvement in welfare legislation which had begun even before the First World War. Controversy has since arisen as to whether the country would not have done better during the war years to have concentrated more upon industrial regeneration rather than the New Jerusalem, despite the social cohesion which promise of the latter engendered. That argument, like the conduct of the war itself, has already produced a considerable literature. Opinions will differ as to the merits of the varying views, but for most of those who lived through the war years, it can be said that they were among the most memorable, if not the happiest, of their lives.

The Posters

1 **You Ought to be Out of London**
Artist: Dudley S Cowes
Printer: J Wiener Ltd, London
29¾″ x 19¾″
INF 13/171/2

2 Famous Last Words
Artist: David Langdon
Printer: Chromoworks Ltd, London
29¼″ x 19¼″
INF 2/73, p.47

3 Women! You are Needed in the National Fire Service
Printer: George Gibbons Ltd, London
29¼″ x 19¾″
INF 13/218/6

4   Look Out in the Blackout
Artist: Pat Kelly
INF 3/290

5   The Life-line is firm thanks to the Merchant Navy
Artist: Charles Wood
Printer: St Michael's Press Ltd, London
38″ x 24¼″
INF 13/213/52

6   To the Merchant Navy: Thank you
Printer: Henry Hildesley Ltd, London
29¾" x 19⅝"
INF 13/213/3

7   To the Merchant Navy: Thank you
Printer: Henry Hildesley Ltd, London
29³/₄″ x 20″
INF 13/213/6

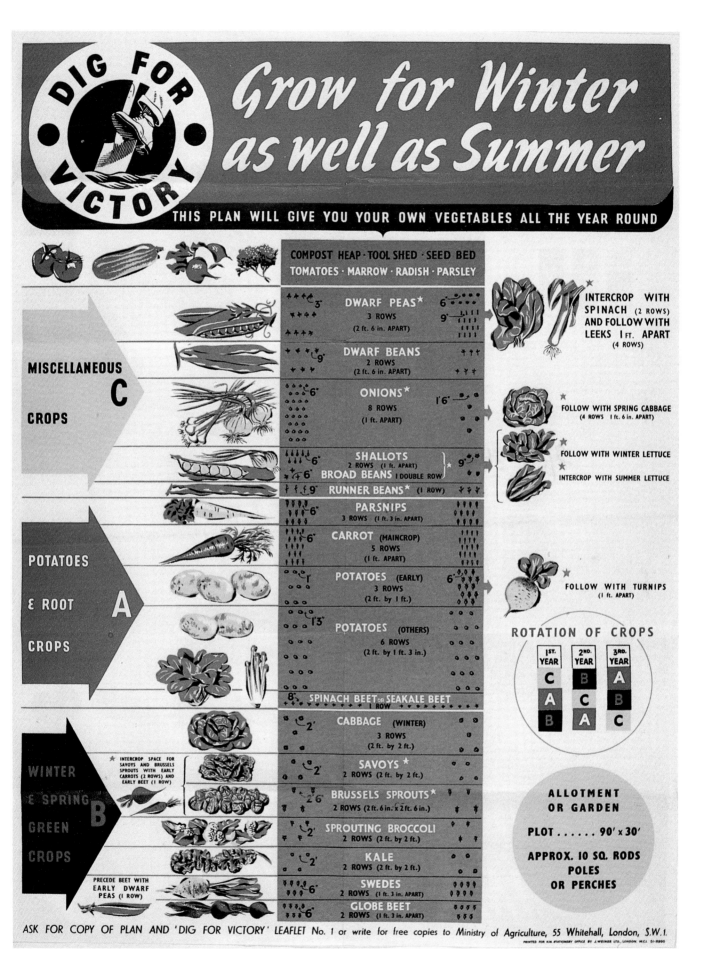

ASK FOR COPY OF PLAN AND 'DIG FOR VICTORY' LEAFLET No. 1 or write for free copies to Ministry of Agriculture, 55 Whitehall, London, S.W.1.

PRINTED FOR H.M. STATIONERY OFFICE BY J.WEINER LTD., LONDON, W.C.1. 51-8990

8   Dig for Victory
Printer: J Weiner Ltd, London
20″ x 25″
MAF 217/5

9 Dig On for Victory
Artist: Peter Fraser
INF 3/96

10   **Join the Women's Land Army**
Printer: Fosh and Cross Ltd, London
30″ x 19½″
INF 13/140/19

11 **Help Scotland's Harvest**
Artist: Conrad T McKenna
Printer: W G Spowart Ltd, Glasgow
29¾″ x 19″
INF 13/140/6

PRINTED FOR H.M. STATIONERY OFFICE BY FOSH & CROSS LTD., LONDON. 51-4949

12 Lend a Hand on the Land
Artist: Showell
Printer: Fosh and Cross Ltd, London
20″ x 15″
INF 13/1430/3

13 Spot at Sight Chart No 1: Enemy Uniforms
Printer: Fosh and Cross Ltd, London
30″ x 20″
INF 13/213/4

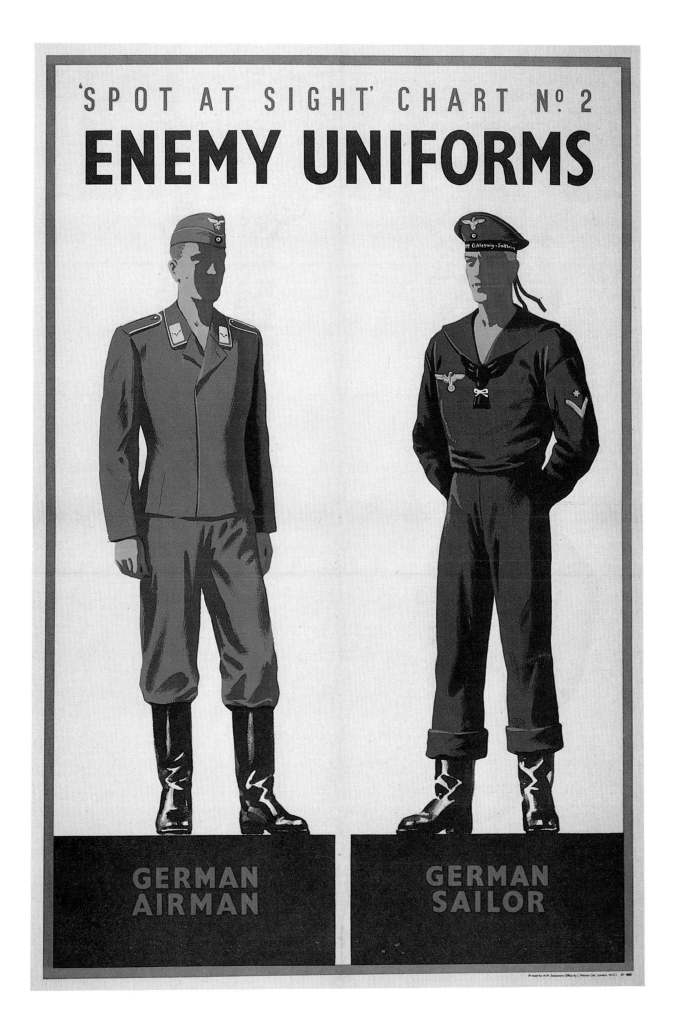

'SPOT AT SIGHT' CHART № 2
ENEMY UNIFORMS

GERMAN AIRMAN

GERMAN SAILOR

14   Spot at 'Sight Chart No 2: Enemy Uniforms
Printer: J Weiner Ltd., London
30″ x 20″
INF 13/213/5

15 **Be Like Dad, Keep Mum**
Artist: Grimes
INF 3/231

16 Careless Talk Costs Lives. Tell nobody - not even her.
14¾" x 9⅞"   EXT 1/119/17

17 Careless Talk Costs Lives. Tell nobody - not even her.
14⅞" x 9⅞"   EXT 1/119/18

18 Careless Talk Costs Lives. Keep Mum - she's not so dumb!
14¾" x 9¾"   EXT 1/119/19

19 Careless Talk Costs Lives. Keep Mum - she's not so dumb!
14⅞" x 9⅞"   EXT 1/119/20

A FEW
CARELESS WORDS
MAY END IN THIS—

Many lives were lost in the last war through careless talk
Be on your guard ! Don't discuss movements of ships or troops

Printed for H.M. Stationery Office by Greycaine Ltd., Watford and London. T 51-5557

20 A Few Careless Words May End in This
Artist: Norman Wilkinson
Printer: Greycaine Ltd, Watford & London
20″ x 14⅞″
INF 13/216/3

21 ATS at the Wheel
Artist: Beverley Pick
Printer: Field Sons & Co. Ltd, Bradford
29¼″ x 19¼″
INF 13/42/8

22 Carry on Canal Workers
Printer: Multi Machine Plates Ltd, London
29$\frac{1}{2}$″ x 19$\frac{1}{2}$″
INF 2/73, p.25

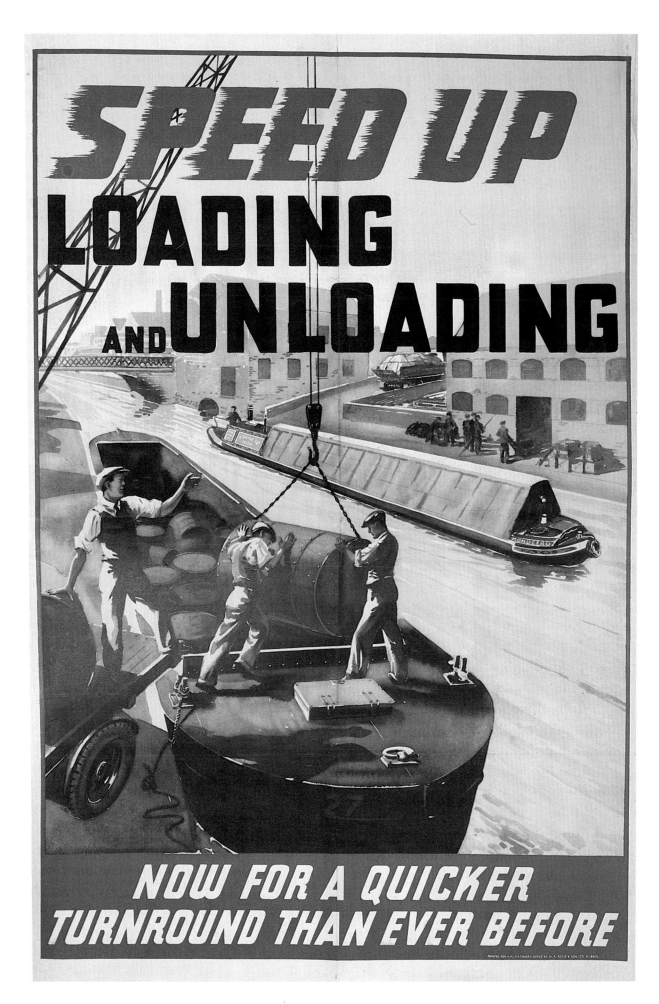

SPEED UP LOADING AND UNLOADING

NOW FOR A QUICKER TURNROUND THAN EVER BEFORE

23 **Speed Up Loading and Unloading**
Printer: W R Royle & Sons Ltd, London
30″ x 20″
INF 2/73, p.23

24 Is Your Journey Really Necessary?
Artist: Bert Thomas
Printer: Haycock Press, London
24¾" x 19¾"
AN 2/126

25 Make Do and Mend
Artist: Donia Nachshen
Printer: W R Royle & Sons Ltd, London
29¾″ x 19¾″
INF 13/144/1

26 Worth Fighting for . . . Worth Saving For
Printer: Field Sons & Co. Ltd, Bradford
28³/₈" x 18⁷/₈"
NSC 5/279

27 Kill Him with War Savings
Printer: J Wiener Ltd, London
30″ x 20″
NSC 5/106

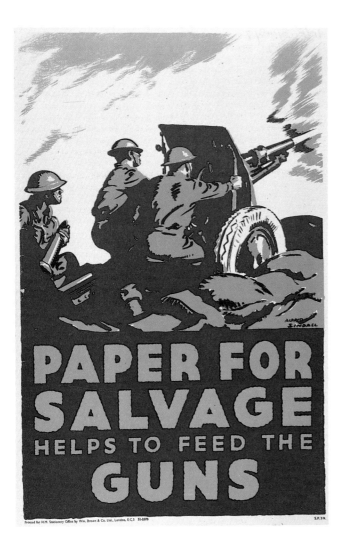

PAPER FOR SALVAGE
HELPS TO FEED THE GUNS

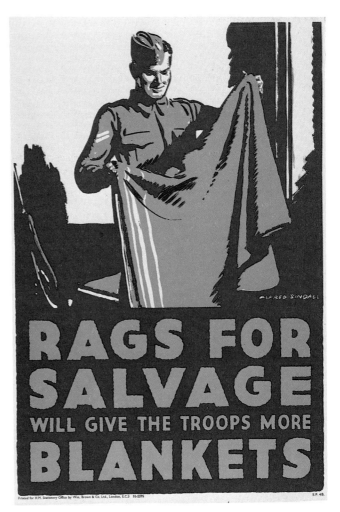

RAGS FOR SALVAGE
WILL GIVE THE TROOPS MORE BLANKETS

"ALL FOR ARMS AND ARMS FOR ALL."

THE THREE SALVAGEERS.

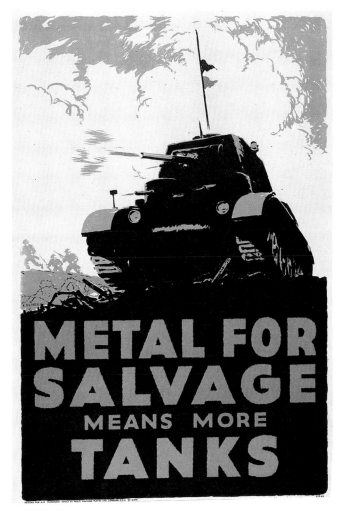

31 **Metal for Salvage means more Tanks**
Artist: E Oliver
Printer: Multi Machine Plates Ltd, London
$14^3/_8$" x $9^3/_4$"
EXT 1/72/9

32 **Rubber for Salvage means more Tyres**
Artist: E Oliver
Printer: George Gibbons Ltd, London
$14^1/_2$" x $9^5/_8$"
EXT 1/72/10

28 **Paper for Salvage helps to feed the Guns**
Artist: Alfred Sindall
Printer: Wm. Brown & Co. Ltd, London
$14^5/_8$" x $9^5/_8$"
EXT 1/72/7

29 **Rags for Salvage will give the troops more blankets**
Artist: Alfred Sindall
Printer: Wm. Brown & Co. Ltd, London
$14^5/_8$" x $9^5/_8$"
EXT 1/72/8

30 **The Three Salvageers**
Artist: Strube
Printer: Flemings, Leicester
$29^1/_2$" x $19^1/_4$"
INF 13/148/9

33 Salvage Saves Shipping
Artist: E Oliver
Printer: George Gibbons Ltd, London
14½″ x 9⅝″
EXT 1/72/6

34 Coughs and Sneezes Spread Diseases
Artist: H M Bateman
Printer: Chromoworks Ltd, London
$29\frac{3}{4}$″ x $19\frac{3}{4}$″
INF 13/18/4

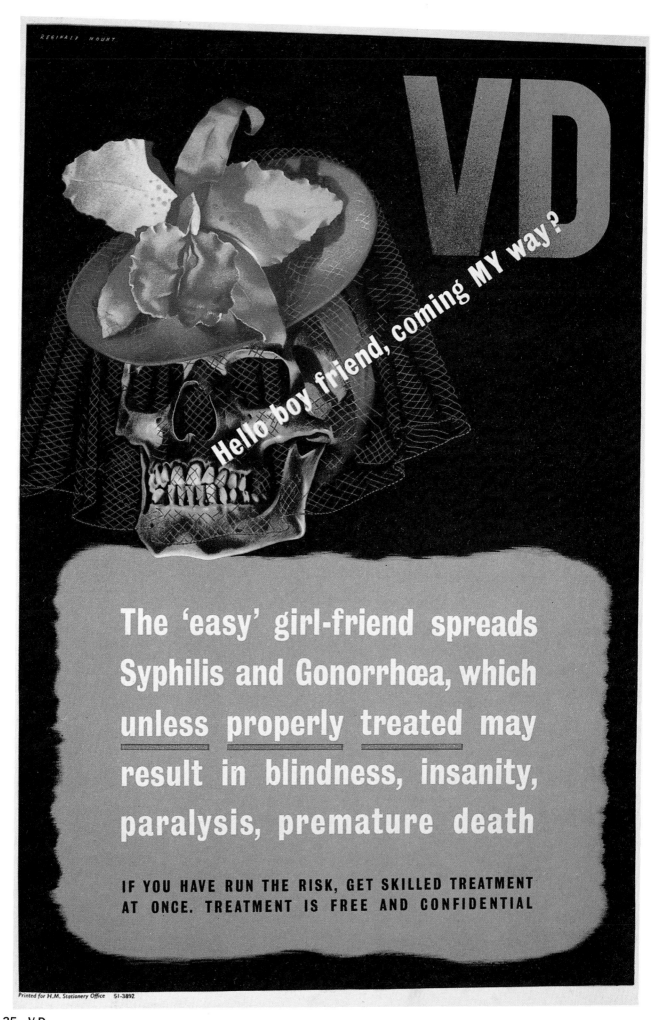

35   V D
Artist: Reginald Mount
13⁷⁄₈″ x 9¹⁄₄″
INF 2/57, p.302

36 [Together]
Artist: Little
INF 3/319

37 **Together**
Printer: Lowe & Brydone Ltd, London
30″ x 20″
INF 2/3, p.277

The British Colonial Empire

ADEN
ANTIGUA
BAHAMAS
BARBADOS
BASUTOLAND
BECHUANALAND PROTECTORATE
BERMUDA
BRITISH GUIANA
BRITISH HONDURAS
BRITISH SOLOMON IS.
BRITISH VIRGIN IS.
CEYLON
CYPRUS
DOMINICA
FALKLAND IS.
FIJI
GAMBIA
GIBRALTAR
GILBERT & ELLICE IS.
GOLD COAST
GRENADA
HONG KONG
JAMAICA
KENYA

MALAYA
MALTA
MAURITIUS
MONTSERRAT
NEW HEBRIDES
NIGERIA
NORTH BORNEO
NORTHERN RHODESIA
NYASALAND
PALESTINE
ST. HELENA
ST. KITTS
ST. LUCIA
ST. VINCENT
SARAWAK
SEYCHELLES
SIERRA LEONE
SOMALILAND
SWAZILAND
TANGANYIKA
TONGA
TRANSJORDAN
TRINIDAD
UGANDA
ZANZIBAR

King's Own Malta Regiment

OUR ALLIES
THE
COLONIES

38 Our Allies the Colonies
Printer: A C Ltd.
29½" x 19¾"
INF 13/213/9

The British Colonial Empire

ADEN	MALAYA
ANTIGUA	MALTA
BAHAMAS	MAURITIUS
BARBADOS	MONTSERRAT
BASUTOLAND	NEW HEBRIDES
BECHUANALAND PROTECTORATE	NIGERIA
BERMUDA	NORTH BORNEO
BRITISH GUIANA	NORTHERN RHODESIA
BRITISH HONDURAS	NYASALAND
BRITISH SOLOMON IS.	PALESTINE
BRITISH VIRGIN IS.	ST. HELENA
CEYLON	ST. KITTS
CYPRUS	ST. LUCIA
DOMINICA	ST. VINCENT
FALKLAND IS.	SARAWAK
FIJI	SEYCHELLES
GAMBIA	SIERRA LEONE
GIBRALTAR	SOMALILAND
GILBERT & ELLICE IS.	SWAZILAND
GOLD COAST	TANGANYIKA
GRENADA	TONGA
HONG KONG	TRANSJORDAN
JAMAICA	TRINIDAD
KENYA	UGANDA
	ZANZIBAR

Royal West African Frontier Force

OUR ALLIES
THE
COLONIES

R.W.A.F.F

Printed in England by A.C. Ltd. 51/2372

39 Our Allies the Colonies
Printer: A C Ltd
29$\frac{1}{2}$" x 19$\frac{3}{4}$"
INF 13/213/10

The British Colonial Empire

ADEN
ANTIGUA
BAHAMAS
BARBADOS
BASUTOLAND
BECHUANALAND PROTECTORATE
BERMUDA
BRITISH GUIANA
BRITISH HONDURAS
BRITISH SOLOMON IS.
BRITISH VIRGIN IS.
CEYLON
CYPRUS
DOMINICA
FALKLAND IS.
FIJI
GAMBIA
GIBRALTAR
GILBERT & ELLICE IS.
GOLD COAST
GRENADA
HONG KONG
JAMAICA
KENYA

MALAYA
MALTA
MAURITIUS
MONTSERRAT
NEW HEBRIDES
NIGERIA
NORTH BORNEO
NORTHERN RHODESIA
NYASALAND
PALESTINE
ST. HELENA
ST. KITTS
ST. LUCIA
ST. VINCENT
SARAWAK
SEYCHELLES
SIERRA LEONE
SOMALILAND
SWAZILAND
TANGANYIKA
TONGA
TRANSJORDAN
TRINIDAD
UGANDA
ZANZIBAR

Ceylon Garrison Artillery

OUR ALLIES THE COLONIES

Printed in England by A.C. Ltd. 51/2372

40 Our Allies the Colonies
Printer: A C Ltd.
29½" x 19¾"
INF 13/213/29

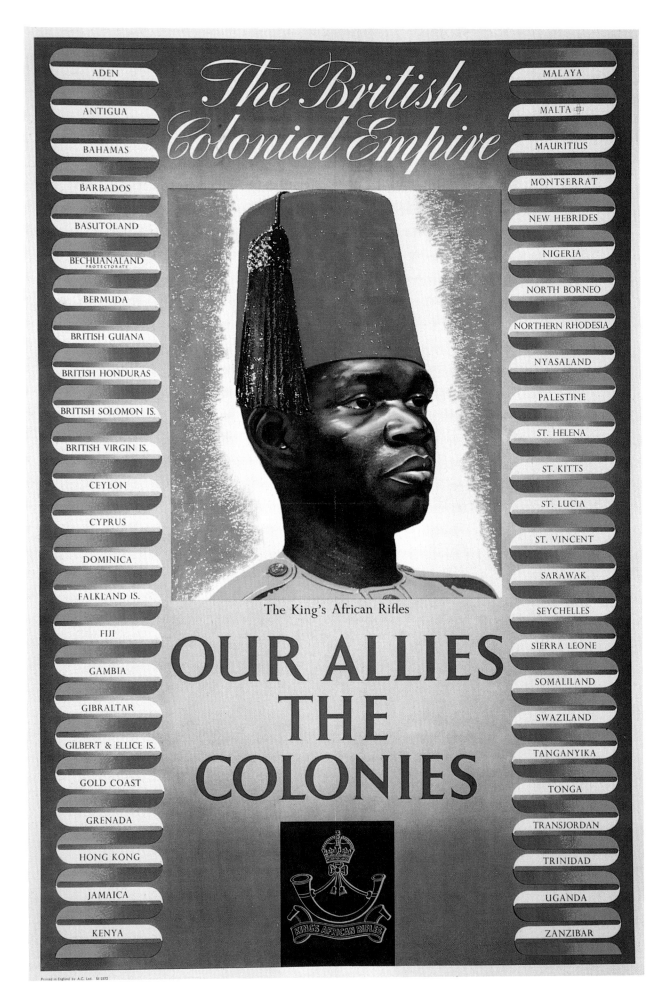

The British Colonial Empire

ADEN	MALAYA
ANTIGUA	MALTA
BAHAMAS	MAURITIUS
BARBADOS	MONTSERRAT
BASUTOLAND	NEW HEBRIDES
BECHUANALAND PROTECTORATE	NIGERIA
BERMUDA	NORTH BORNEO
BRITISH GUIANA	NORTHERN RHODESIA
BRITISH HONDURAS	NYASALAND
BRITISH SOLOMON IS.	PALESTINE
BRITISH VIRGIN IS.	ST. HELENA
CEYLON	ST. KITTS
CYPRUS	ST. LUCIA
DOMINICA	ST. VINCENT
FALKLAND IS.	SARAWAK
FIJI	SEYCHELLES
GAMBIA	SIERRA LEONE
GIBRALTAR	SOMALILAND
GILBERT & ELLICE IS.	SWAZILAND
GOLD COAST	TANGANYIKA
GRENADA	TONGA
HONG KONG	TRANSJORDAN
JAMAICA	TRINIDAD
KENYA	UGANDA
	ZANZIBAR

The King's African Rifles

OUR ALLIES THE COLONIES

Printed in England by A.C. Ltd. 51-3372

41 Our Allies the Colonies
Printer: A C Ltd
29½″ x 19¾″
INF 13/213/31

42 Unless we can divide those two fellows - we're sunk!
INF 3/322

RUSSIA'S FIGHT

TRANSLATION   *Kill the Fascist Reptile!*

TRANSLATION   *The enemy will be mercilessly defeated and*

43   Russia's Fight is Ours!
39³⁄₄″ x 19³⁄₈″
INF 13/123/19

S OURS !

These posters from Moscow show the determination of our Ally to destroy Hitlerite Germany. But with a large part of their industrial resources already overrun they desperately need our help. Production is the key. Russia's fight is ours and **OUR FIGHT IS RUSSIA'S**

СМЕРТЬ
ФАШИСТСКОЙ
ГАДИНЕ!

TRANSLATION *Death to the Fascist Reptile!*

НАПОЛЕОН ПОТЕРПЕЛ ПОРАЖЕНИЕ.
ТО ЖЕ БУДЕТ И С ЗАЗНАВШИМСЯ
ГИТЛЕРОМ!

1812.

TRANSLATION *Napoleon failed and so will that blackguard Hitler!*

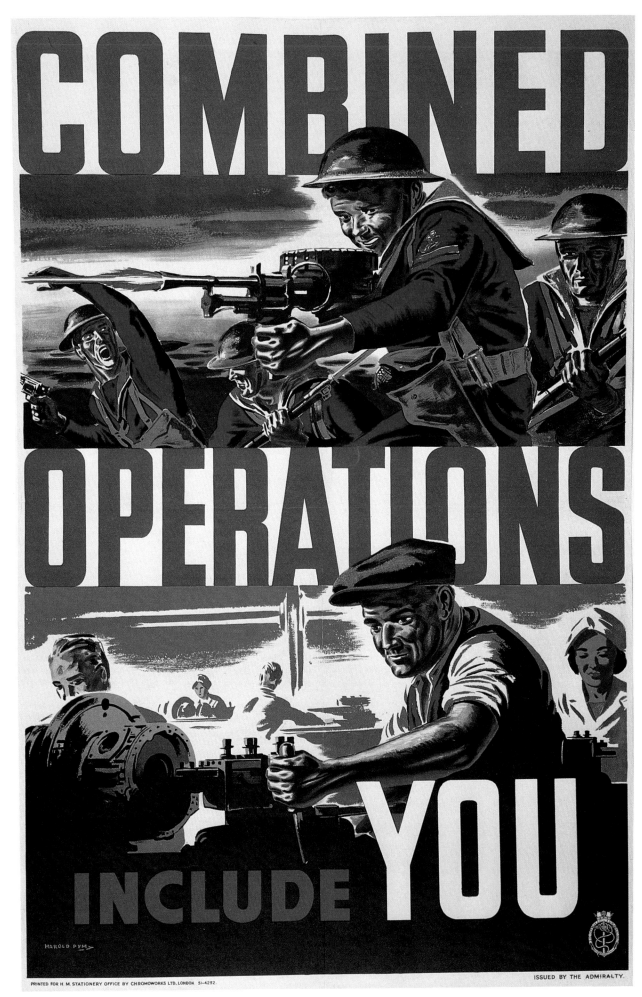

44 Combined Operations Include You
Artist: Harold Pym
Printer: Chromoworks Ltd, London
29³⁄₄″ x 19³⁄₄″
INF 13/213/21

45 Women of Britain — Come into the Factories
Artist: Zec
Printer: Lowe & Brydone Ltd, London
29¼" x 19¼"
INF 13/126/6

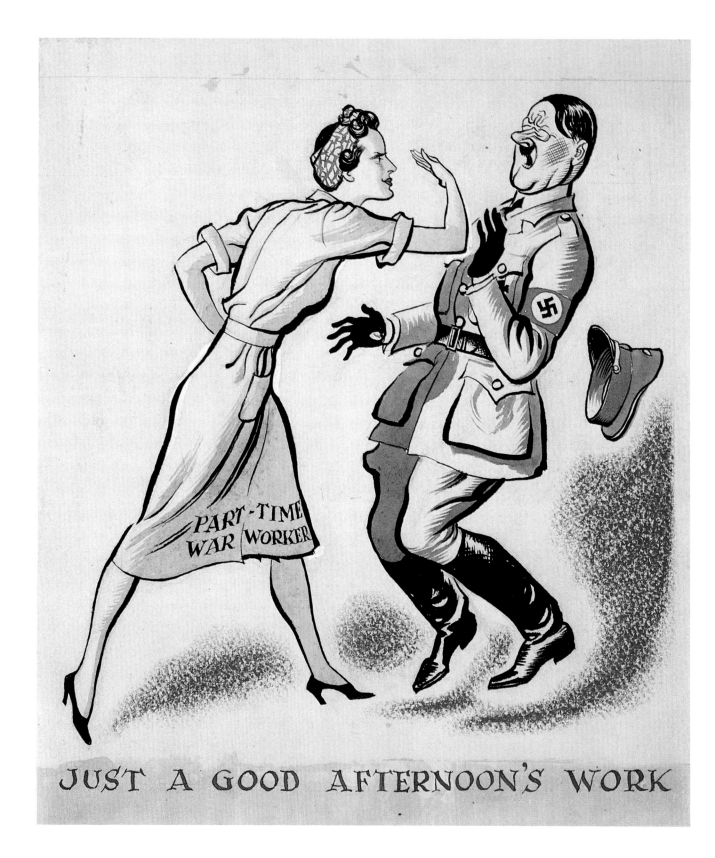

JUST A GOOD AFTERNOON'S WORK

46   Just a Good Afternoon's Work
INF 3/400

The big raids on Germany continue.   British war plants share with the R.A.F. credit for these giant operations.

THE ATTACK
BEGINS IN THE FACTORY

G.P. 3/15/6.

PRINTED IN ENGLAND by CHROMOWORKS LTD LONDON. 51-4265.

47   The Attack Begins in the Factory
Artist: Roy Nockolds
Printer: Chromoworks Ltd, London
29½" x 19⅝"
INF 13/123/6

The new Airborne Army is now in action in Europe—equipped by British factories.

THE ATTACK BEGINS IN THE FACTORY

48   The Attack Begins in the Factory
Artist: Oliphant
Printer: Thomas Forman & Sons Ltd, Nottingham
30″ x 19¾″
INF 13/123/14

With depth charges, guns and ammunition from British factories Allied submarines have wrought havoc among Axis shipping in the Mediterranean.

THE ATTACK BEGINS IN THE FACTORY

49 **The Attack Begins in the Factory**
Artist: Gilbert Rumbold
Printer: Chromoworks Ltd, London
29¾" x 19⅝"
INF 13/123/7

50 Full Ahead Production
Artist: Pat Keely
Printer: Multi Machine Plates Ltd, London
29½" x 19¾"
INF 13/122/5

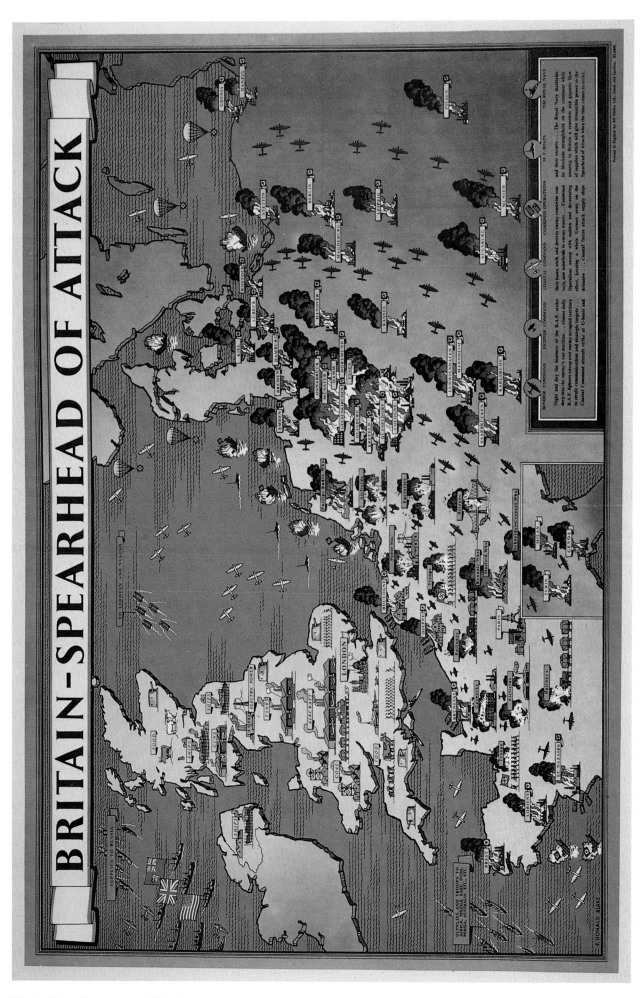

51 Britain: Spearhead of Attack
Artist: F Donald Blake
Printer: Alf Cooks Ltd, Leeds & London
29³/₄″ x 9¹/₂″
INF 13/213/42

A British cruiser ramming an Italian submarine in the Mediterranean

BACK THEM UP!

52   Back Them Up!
Artist: Marc Stone
Printer: James Haworth and Brother Ltd, London
29³/₄″ x 20″
INF 13/123/24

Heavy "Stirling" bombers raid the Nazi Baltic port of Lübeck and leave the docks ablaze

BACK THEM UP!

PRINTED FOR H.M. STATIONERY OFFICE BY FOSH & CROSS LTD., LONDON (51-2438)

53 Back Them Up!
Artist: Roy Nockolds
Printer: Fosh and Cross Ltd, London
29″ x 19″
INF 13/123/22

British guns blast a way through Axis defences in North Africa

BACK THEM UP !

PRINTED FOR H.M. STATIONERY OFFICE BY FOSH & CROSS LTD., LONDON. 51-3409

54 **Back Them Up!**
Artist: Nunney
Printer: Fosh and Cross Ltd, London
29¾" x 19½"
INF 13/213/41

A British tank attack in the Western Desert

BACK THEM UP!

PRINTED IN ENGLAND BY FOSH & CROSS LTD., LONDON. (51-2400)

55 Back Them Up!
Printer: Fosh and Cross Ltd, London
29³/₄" x 20"
INF 13/123/25

The Mediterranean Invasion. British troops, tanks and guns pouring ashore from landing craft.

BACK THEM UP!

56 Back Them Up!
Printer: Thomas Forman & Sons Ltd, Nottingham
29¾" x 19¾"
INF 13/123/5

"Hurricanes" of the Royal Air Force co-operating with the Russian Air Force.

BACK THEM UP!

PRINTED IN ENGLAND by CHROMOWORKS LTD LONDON. 51-2326.

57 Back Them Up!
Artist: Jobson
Printer: Chromoworks Ltd, London
29³⁄₄″ x 19⁵⁄₈″
INF 13/123/21

LIBYA

Help them finish the job

PRINTED FOR H.M. STATIONERY OFFICE BY THE BRITISH COLOUR PRINTING C⁰ L.ᵀᴰ 51-9570.

58 **Libya: Help them finish the job**
Printer: British Colour Printing Company Ltd, London
30½" x 20½"
INF 13/213/45

LIBYA
Help them finish the job

PRINTED FOR H.M. STATIONERY OFFICE BY FOSH & CROSS LTD., LONDON.   51-9569

59 Libya: Help them finish the job
Artist: Wootton
Printer: Fosh and Cross Ltd, London
30″ x 20″
INF 13/213/44

LIBYA
Help them finish the job

60 **Libya: Help them finish the job**
Artist: Marc Stone
Printer: Fosh and Cross Ltd, London
30" x 19¾"
INF 13/213/53

61 **This is the Year: Its up to us to let 'em have it**
Artist: Clive Upton
Printer: Field Sons & Co. Ltd, Bradford
39″ x 29″
INF 13/122/6

Great Britain will pursue the WAR AGAINST JAPAN to the very end.

WINSTON CHURCHILL

Printed in England by J. Howitt & Son Ltd., Nottm.   51-1290

62   War Against Japan
Printer: J Howitt & Sons Ltd, Nottingham
29³/₄" x 19³/₄"
INF 13/213/12

Great Britain will pursue the WAR AGAINST JAPAN to the very end.

WINSTON CHURCHILL

Printed in England by J. Howitt & Son Ltd., Nottm.   51-1290

63   War Against Japan
Printer: J Howitt & Sons Ltd, Nottingham
29⁷⁄₈″ x 19³⁄₄″
INF 13/213/14

64   War Against Japan
Printer: J Howitt & Son Ltd, Nottingham
29⁷/₈″ x 19³/₄″
INF 13/213/15

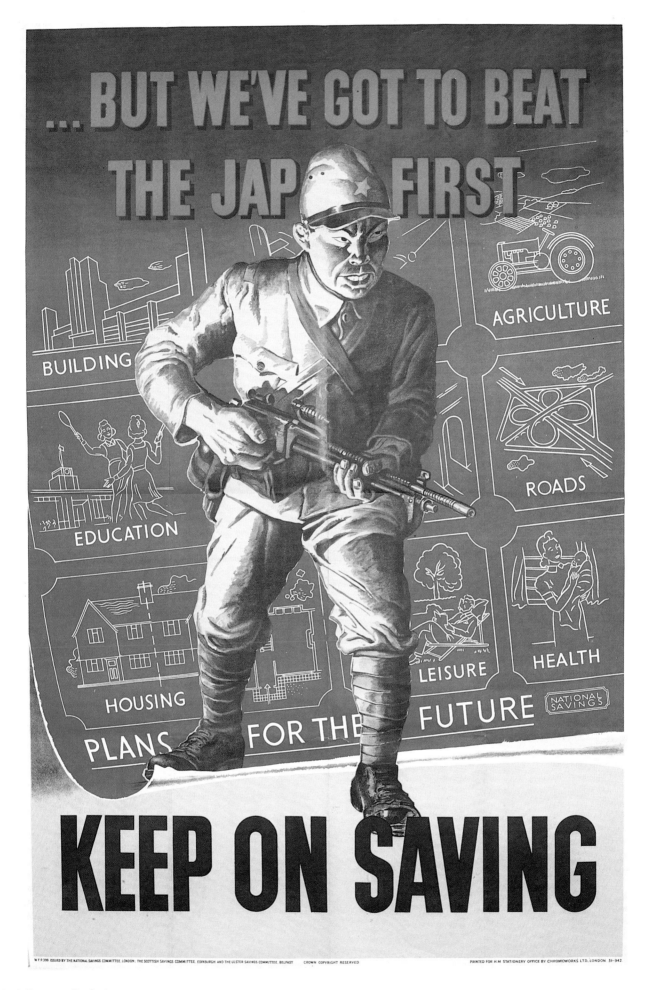

65   Keep on Saving
Printer: Chromoworks Ltd, London
59$\frac{1}{2}$" x 39$\frac{3}{4}$"
NSC 5/139